AWAKENING

ELIZABETH JOY

First Printing 1987
Second Printing 1988
Third Printing 1990

Copyright©1987
Elizabeth Joy Productions
P.O. Box 4507
Taos, New Mexico 87571

Cover Illustration: Ashisha
Typography: Pioneer Graphics

I dedicate this book to the divine spirit, moving through all, and to those of you who have had the courage to surrender to its love.

To your own opening. . .

What is happening on Earth today is a balancing, an equalizing of energy — a relaxation into awareness of essence, of spirit that has always been and always will be. Feeling the smooth vitality of spirit as it flows through us swiftly, calmly, and peacefully, our place is to listen elegantly to the song, to understand and feel the unspoken word within.

This book is a tribute to the spiritual awakening that is taking place on our planet today. In my perception, spirituality is the realization that we each hold within all of the necessary tools, creativity, and light to make our journey a fulfilling, prosperous, and loving one.

The illusion that exists on our Earth is that there is no essence behind what we see. The truth is, all that there is, is essence, some of which has slowed itself down to form.

The time has truly come for seeing deeper and hearing clearer, for looking beyond our own life, to embrace the similarities instead of the differences. We, as a whole consciousness on earth are being given the ways and the inspiration to do so, and that is so very beautiful. We have learned that making peace in our outer world comes from making peace within.

We are at a time when we must do our part to awaken the earth, and we each must begin with ourselves. It is vital. Peace and Blessings.

Elizabeth Joy
1987

CONTENTS

CHAPTER 1
INTUITION:
THE GIFT OF LIGHT

---

*Your intuition is one of your
most natural, most beautiful,
and most powerful ways
of communication.*

You are given this gift to tune into any situation
you feel you need some information from. This is a
way of letting you know that there is a bridge that
goes beyond space and time. This bridge enables your
future self to help you reach greater love in the present as well as enabling you to help your past self

reach greater love through your knowledge in the present.

Space and time are boundaries only if you believe them to be.

There are many other planes where space and time are nonexistent, where your entity is regarded in its totality, and all of your incarnations on this planet and others are understood to be an amalgam of who you are. Each experience is viewed as a necessary and natural prerequisite for the next. When you have fully learned what an experience has to teach you, there is a healthy release. Lessons of enjoyment are equally as important as lessons of discernment and wisdom. It takes wisdom to be carefree and to enjoy. It takes wisdom to know when to let up on the reigns of serious moods and balance them with lightness and laughter. It takes wisdom to know the kinds of environments that suit you best, that heal you the most, and delight your senses and your spirit. It takes wisdom to walk in balance. Your intuition is your channel to inner wisdom. It brings you the most pertinent and valid information.

For example, when you walk into a room or think of certain colors, or visit certain people, you are instantly receiving messages as to which things are the most healing for you. The information will come through your 'body-knowing,' that amazingly clear channel within that is made up of thousands of nerves and muscles, all needing peace, relaxation, and light to function at their best. Your body is the greatest tool you have. When your body feels other than at its best, pay attention to what has taken place, to where you have been, to who you have been with and to what your thoughts were.

Your intuition comes to you through your thoughts or through your body-knowing.

When you use your intuition, you are tapping into the planes where space and time are non-existent. Intuition is a natural quality that all people will make use of in the coming years and that more and more of you who are sensitive are already working with. Information that comes from other realms is received telepathically through your being, much in the same way that information from this earthly realm is received.

Your soul-guides and your own higher self have the ability to see beyond space and time, to know of events happening in another part of the earth, transcending space, or in the future or past, transcending time. You will receive this information if it is for your highest and most healing good to know the information. If you can use it in some way to help yourself to grow and to evolve, you will be tapped into the information.

Many people want to know how to make communication with guides. It is not a matter of how to get the guides to communicate, but how to clear your own mind to be able to listen. To just listen. It is in the stillness that the power moves. It is in the stillness that the words ring through.

---

*Be still and you will hear,
or see or sense or just simply know.*

All ways of receiving are valid. Not everyone has motion pictures in their heads. Some do, others have a deep feeling. When you learn to trust and follow these feelings, you begin to build a gentle rapport with those beings of light who come in service and in love.

It is not necessarily important to personify the energies of guides that surround you. To personify can be limiting, as each energy has had a very large number of incarnations in so many realms, so that to call a guide "Sam" limits you to a single persona and incarnation or existence. Again we come to the idea of perceiving each entity as a whole being. Each lifetime is a drop in the bucket. To expand your vision to this perception puts you in touch with something greater and more expansive than your everyday inherited reality. While it is true that you choose your reality, there are those in your life who have chosen the same reality before you, and you have picked up certain perceptions from them. There is a world of difference between the fact that you choose your reality and knowing consciously that you choose your reality. Knowing this allows your decisions to be your own. It allows your decisions to be conscious ones.

Though the guides and teachers and beings of light are always willing to help, it is also necessary to invite them lovingly, much as you do an honored guest. There are various ways to do the inviting. One, as I mentioned, is to take quiet time. The invisible realms find it quite difficult to give you information and guidance if you are constantly moving, thinking, talking, or working.

*Taking time for yourself,
where you can be open and
receptive to the
impressions of your soul,
is a very healing
thing to do.*

The reality of those in the invisible realms is not linear, so you may not receive your information at the exact time of asking, but if you have created a space of silence and receptivity, you can know that the guides will tune into that opening when it is appropriate that you receive something.

*As long as your intention is
to heal, the high inner worlds
will begin to open up for you,
showing you ways, words, and
actions that are truly healing.*

So often you envision seeking to be active. Some of the most effective seeking can be passive. A passive state is a receptive one. It is one in which all of your chakra centers and sensory faculties are alert and yet relaxed, open and yet wise.

Wisdom allows you the quality of discernment, the discernment which tells you which thoughts of yours are creative and healing and which would best be released. Your wisdom also helps you to identify which thoughts you have picked up from other people during energy exchanges during the day. Just by thinking of someone, you can pick up their thoughts and their energy. In order to avoid taking on any low vibrations in a public place, where there are so many thoughts floating around, or from someone who is feeling down, begin to send out loving vibrations.

Allow yourself the freedom to choose love.

When you send out love and healing thoughts, you cannot be affected by other people's negativity. Love is more powerful than negativity, and wipes it out. Sending love helps to raise others' vibrations and you end up feeling much more peaceful and at ease with yourself.

*To give love
is to have love.*

Love truly is a cleanser and a mender.

Love heals.

Become aware when you begin to feel down, and start broadcasting mountains of quiet sunshine to those around you or to those in your thoughts. You have thousands of thoughts in a single day. Your wisdom allows you to see the connection between what you think of and what is actually taking place in your life.

*Your thoughts are creating
your reality every moment
of every day.*

INTUITION: THE GIFT OF LIGHT

As you begin to become aware of your thoughts, your vibration changes. As you pay attention to your thoughts and guide them to higher levels, your vibration begins to rise. You begin to feel good about feeling responsible for yourself and your own choices. The truth is, you choose all that you do and say and are. The more you understand this truth, the more self power you can cultivate.

By increased self power, I am speaking of confidence and trust in yourself and in your path, and respect and love for your self. This is a much softer view of power than has been put forth in the past.

To honor and delight
in yourself allows you to be
the healing light for
all others you connect with.

CHAPTER 2
FORGIVENESS:
THE PATH OF PEACE

When you choose to live on the earth plane and experience physical life, you do so to move through lessons and create growth which leads you towards increased unconditional love. Total unconditional love coupled with the depths of wisdom is your ultimate goal.

Forgiveness is one of the greatest tools you have to help you open to your inner wisdom and intuition, and take you toward greater love in your life.

*Forgiveness is a
cleansing power. It is
love and light in action.*

By consciously choosing to forgive past actions that may not have seemed to be for your highest good, or may have seemed to hinder you along your path of light in some way, you set up a clearance of any energy you are holding onto, and by releasing it from your auric field, you no longer draw to you the same kinds of situations.

You know the feeling of wanting to release something so much, that you dwell upon it, only to draw it in again. You draw the same situations, sometimes with different actors and actresses, sometimes with the same ones.

As many times during the day as you can think to do so, the act of forgiving frees you from fear and transforms your doubts into love, light, and prosperous wonder.

When you feel free from fear, you can open your heart and experience self love. When you can open your heart, inner knowing, or sensing energy, or the use of your intuitive faculty becomes abundantly available to you.

Sensing energy is done through the heart.

Safety is the issue we are speaking of when we speak of opening the heart. Sometimes in your childhood or through various relationships in your teenage or adult years, you were given the telepathic or verbal message that it was not safe to open your heart — that if you did, you would become vulnerable, feel hurt or inadequate. You are relearning that as part of your path of light, self love allows you to surrender. Self love allows you to be open to all energies without necessarily taking them in and being affected by them if they do not seem to be loving and wise. As you become in charge of your own life, you are able to release others to be in charge of their own lives and make their own wondrous decisions. You can release situations, people, or energies that are not resonating with the high parts of your being. You begin to listen to your soul instead of your ego.

As you begin to see below the surface of your past experiences enough to reap the benefits, a nicer rapport begins to develop with yourself. You become filled with acceptance of where you have been, who you have been, and most of all, what you can bring to the present moment.

The rose begins to emerge from the thorns.

Just as the rose will bloom, the human will open to love.

You begin to have a fuller understanding of how to appreciate the present moment as it unfolds before you, offering itself to you, and you are free to choose, to know what your inner being wants to experience, and how it wants to experience it.

It is only your past that brings up your fears, for the present is full of love.

Love lives in the moment.

When you hold your past up to the light of your soul, the negativity fades away and allows the soul's guidance to step in. You can send blessings into your past to clear it up.

Our essence is not linear.

Our essence emcompasses all time while being time-less.

Your fears simply need love and acceptance. Do not run from your fears. That only makes them more afraid. They truly are as little children. You can feel your fears in your physical body and if they are not paid attention to, they solidify into physical pain. Physical pain is fear that has manifested in form.

The greatest thing you can do to alleviate your fears is to recognize and accept them.

Your fears are there for a reason. They are seeking your attention to tell you an important message about an unresolved conflict you have created in order to grow and learn more about yourself and, most importantly, to learn more about love.

Becoming whole and loving yourself involves acknowledging these fears that are reaching out to you in the best way they know how. Begin to visualize

15

these fears bathed in light, becoming gentle, telling you what lessons they have to offer and what growth they are producing for you. Love them for helping you and thank yourself for helping them, and then let them go, back to their essence of love.

Gratitude is a powerful energy that draws to you more of what you are grateful for.

Some of you feel tied to your past through your desire to figure it all out. Know that you can never figure it all out. Life is one big, divine orchestration. The violin player does not read the cellist's notes; she simply enjoys the harmony that they are creating. And so for you, your past was one movement in your life, it had ups and it had downs. That polarity is the nature of earth plane reality, but do not think for one moment that you are necessarily bound to your past. That was your own decision. The Creator has let it go. Understand that it is not going to get any better, or any worse, because 'better' and 'worse' are your creations! Because our essence is not linear, it is all here now! The truth of the moment is that it is totally pregnant with aliveness, and at the same time, it is totally empty. It is all here now. All that has ever been and all that ever will be, is here NOW. The stiller you become, the more you will know this. You have decided that if you change, you will be better. Why? Why? You are who you are. Rejoice and be grateful for that. All that you do is a part of God.

Knowing God transcends all Karma.

Love yourself.

Becoming whole is a process and your intuition reveals the steps to you one at a time.

The light of your soul is constantly shining for you, showing you that in essence you truly are whole, filled with wonder and dance and spontaneity.

Your soul is showing you who you truly are — a spark of divine light manifest in form.

Your soul encourages and supports you as you take the time and inner memory to discover your power, and share your love. For this sharing is your birthright.

Go home to your soul and reach your beauty-filled inner self.

CHAPTER 3
RELATIONSHIPS

Relationships are one of the most powerful tools we have on earth to learn about ourselves, about each other, and to begin our journey home toward the Light.

Remaining open to your feelings is one of the best ways to learn about your inner self.

Many of you feel excited and confused around the issue of relationships, especially at how to create and sustain the loving relationship that you feel in your hearts. Those of you who create or deepen a bond between you and another being, will ultimately and joyously be deepening the bond between you and yourself.

Without deepening your relationship to yourself, it is difficult to relate to others. Relationships provide a mirror, a reflection of who you are and how you relate to the world around you. They are gifts to you from the depths of your being. Any shadow areas or patterns you have in your life will be brought to light by relationship.

When two people commit to loving and growing together, whether it be partners, family, or friends, they have also committed to unraveling the mystery and power within and discovering a journey of infinite love and compassion.

We all need love. Don't be too proud to ask for it, or to know that it is what makes you tick. A loving relationship is built on trust, mutual respect, caring, and openess. When you open yourself up to another in a loving relationship, you will find that all parts of your being are acceptable. To accept the other person unconditionally is a vital part of closeness. To hold that person in the highest esteem, despite their flaws, allows them to feel safe and comfortable. To feel alive and young at heart comes from good relationships.

Laughter! Sense of humour, and joke-making are so important in love.

Give a good chuckle! Laugh deep and well and with love.

Mutual support is a part of every relationship that works. Love the other. Do not let your ego get in the way of love. Your ego will carry on and on until it gets its way. Love sees all possibilities. Love feels safe. It does not need to fight to get its way. Be a friend to the other. Realize the good between you.

Love forgives again and again, and yet again.

Start with whomever you know and be a friend. You have taken yourself too seriously when you cannot find a way to be a friend.

Release your defenses; they are not you.

Step out of your own self and reach out . . . Care! It feels so good. Start with your children. Please! They certainly deserve support, trust, and special caring. Children are our precious links to the future and the incandescent doorway to the everlasting present. Your children are able to awaken within you that which you already know and feel, and sometimes have forgotten. To affirm to your children what they already know is the greatest gift you can give to them. Affirm their feelings, their love, their words. Enhance their sense of self love. What we give with love, to the children, they hold so gracefully. They are close to the divine in their purity of thought, close to the divine in their purity of speech, and we should be grateful for their examples.

Love the animals. Look in to your animal's eyes and see. . . love. Animals reflect back to us so much warmth and softness. They reveal to us our nurturing nature, and our desire to care. Animals speak to us through feelings, through telepathic communication, and through inner knowing.

Those of you who feel the need to create an intimate relationship in your lives, must also remember that the divine plan is fulfilling itself. And, if you have chosen to be alone at this time, it is to understand the power that lies within your own being. Once you master this understanding, you are free from all delusions about spending time alone and you can begin using it to your advantage.

God opens millions of flowers each day and moves the ocean tide in perfect rhythm; you can also be sure that your life is fulfilling itself in its perfect, unique, divine rhythm.

Leave everything to
its own destiny.

Those of you who are in relationships are in them because they mirror a part of you that you need to see. I will give you a simple exercise to demonstrate this. Write down ten qualities that you see in a person you are in relationship with, and you will see that you either find these qualities within yourself, or at some deep level you would like to manifest or change these qualities within you.

Those of you who are in relationships where judgement is involved, look at the thing you are judging. You will find that you either possess the same thing and would like to change it, or you simply have a judgement against it. Perhaps you manifest the total opposite of that quality now, because in the past, possibly in another lifetime, you manifested the quality you so dislike. Remember, you did not create these qualities, you chose to channel them through you to act out certain parts, and to learn certain lessons. (Those of you manifesting illness are doing so to give yourself the chance, in the face of discomfort and pain to overcome that pain courageously, and to love despite it.)

We are all connected. The more you heal yourself, the more you are healing the forcefield of energy surrounding the planet, and the more you will draw healing to you and to those around you. A relationship can be a very healing bond if you allow it be. Allowance is a powerful idea in relationship. Allowing the other person to be who they are, to come from where they are at, be at a place of joy, agony, or uncertainty shows a deep level of trust and understanding. When you are clear about allowing yourself and the other to be who you are, you will find a much different rhythm developing between you.

When you tap into the natural rhythm, as opposed to imposing one of your own, you are tapping into the divine interplay that will unfold itself before you, and that — is magical.

Clarity in your life in all areas will help you greatly in relationship. The clarity of knowing the essence of what it is you desire, allows you to know if you have it or not, and it allows you to know when it comes along. We are speaking of essences, rather than form, because essence is God's creation, and form is the creation of your ego. Attention is the essence you may desire, but a new car will not ultimately fulfill this desire, so your higher self sends along a friend, a good friend, and you think, "Gee, I wish I had an intimate relationship in my life." Well, that may not be what you truly need at this time. If it was, you would have it.

A most effective way to create the qualities you desire in a relationship is to become deeply in touch with those qualities yourself. To become in touch with these qualities, you will need to know specifically what they are. You will need to know how they feel. You will need to spend some time experiencing the qualities you so desire. For example, if you desire safety, knowingness, tolerance, and carefreeness, you will need to generate these qualities first in your own being while you are alone. Then you have a reference, a feeling to compare with what you are feeling when you encounter another. It shifts the process from the mind to the feelings, an imbalance which greatly needs balancing.

It is very easy to speak truth, but to enliven it inside so that you are bursting with joy and delight — that is living the ultimate truth.

Many times you will enter a relationship based on your mental process. Thoughts like — well he seems nice, he likes birds and I like birds, he loves sushi and so do I — may satisfy you mentally, but may or may not satisfy your feeling, or intuitive nature. Your intuition may be saying something much different. Pay attention and you will know.

Still your being, your entire body and mind, and listen.

Receive. . . yourself. Stilling yourself lets you know what is inherently yours.

Everyone that you encounter provides you with an energy exchange and a chance to watch your own reactions, feelings, judgements, and acceptances. The moment you begin to feel responsible for your reactions, for the way you interact with people, energies, and situations, is the moment you are one very essential step closer to home. If you feel heavily influenced by another person, or people in your lives, in a way that feels negative to you, the way to begin to release that influence, is to take responsibility for accepting it in the first place. There are no victims, and you are no exception. It takes at least two, one to give and one to receive. When you decide to look solely for the divine in everything you encounter, in every eye you meet, you will draw that to you! It is not some abstract idea. What you think about, is what you attract. Watch it, examine your lives. Please. There is not one other person on this earth who can take the job of your personal introspection and do it for you. Introspection means going within, and until you do, you will be at the mercy of people, energies, and situations, as opposed to realizing that you can and do choose all of the time. Some of you have chosen NOT to choose and then feel miserable with your lives.

> *You are the master of your own life.*

There is always more to learn and deeper to go. It begins with taking responsibility for who you are.

CHAPTER 4
REFLECTION

All that you experience in this life is a mirror reflection of who you are. That is the nature of earth plane reality. You are comprised of energy, and like attracts like, so you will resonate with things that are already a part of you. Many of you wonder about your relationship to money, and how to attract it in your lives. Money is energy. You must create a rapport with your self worth in order to create energy lines moving toward you and away from you as well, for balance — giving and receiving.

Abundance is yours when
you believe it to be.

AWAKENING

The energy of abundance is about you, your world, and the way you perceive your relationship to all of the things in it, based on how you perceive yourself. When you perceive the world around you to be giving, loving, and providing, it is a reflection of the fact that you perceive yourself to be wise and loving and worthy. When you shut off this flow, it is usually because you have decided upon an image for yourself which is less than wise, loving, and deserving. Give yourself the opportunity to be open to the infinite possibilities of life, awareness, and love. Allow it to take you to the inner depths of your being to come up with new and opportune ways to fulfill your own divine destiny.

The austerities of the past, memories of lifetimes spent as ascetics, or monks, are still with many of you. Realize that you can be spiritual and enjoy life on earth. The way to the divinity within is through the balancing of the high angelic energies with the deep earth energies. The interplay between the two is what makes for wholeness, openess, and oneness with the present moment. Are you aware that the next person you see is a part of God? Are you aware of the sounds and smells and sights around you? Are you aware of the colors and textures around you?

Become aware.

REFLECTION

Begin to notice what kinds of things draw you in. Watch what makes you feel alive, centered, and powerful. These feelings are the voice from your higher self letting you know that the things that make you feel this way are the things you should be doing. This is a sure way to know who you are, what your energy field consists of, and what you enjoy.

When you are taken in by an emotion, a story, a feeling, it is your own. Somewhere inside of you, you also have this emotion or feeling. When we come to understand the truth of reflection, there is another level to this that must also be experienced and this is the old adage "putting yourself in another's shoes." This idea is as old as the wind, and yet it is truly the advanced soul who can apply this while maintaining his or her own center. Once you have truly experienced who you are, having seen yourself with your own eyes, there is another wonderful step to deepening this process. That step is to accept all parts of your brothers and sisters and all parts of yourself that may seem to challenge, or uncenter you. The next true step in coming to terms with your own wholeness is to seek it out. Seek out the rough edges so that they can be polished. Rejoice in your growth. Do take it seriously, but not with heavy graveness, for it is all God.

All that is, is part of God.

After all, it is quite easy to deeply love a loving being. The masters are masters because they have learned the one spiritual truth you are all looking for and that is that it is all inside of each individual, so whether you shall love them or not, and whether you shall accept them or not, the masters stand as love. They stand as an example of self acceptance. Understand that not you or any human being will be accepted one hundred percent of the time. Once you really understand this, much of the deeply-seated pressure you carry around with you to be accepted all of the time will dissipate.

If you accept yourself just as you are, what others say will not be so important.

If you do not accept yourself as you truly are, all of the approval in the world could not truly make you feel happy. The time and the energy that you give to yourself is the most important gift you can learn to use well. The more you accept yourself the more acceptance you will find in the outer world. And when you do not feel accepted in the outer world, as sometimes happens, you will have a reservoir of self-acceptance from which to drink and nourish yourself. You will no longer take it to heart. Remember, everything is an expression of love or a cry for it, so if you feel nonacceptance coming at you, out of the depth of your being, you will recognize it as a call and begin to broadcast just what the other person truly needs. Like attracts like. Your soul self is gentle; it doesn't need to prove itself to you or to anybody else. It speaks softly and lovingly, suggesting what it knows to be best for you, rather than demanding it.

> *Your soul sees no need to defend itself, for it feels its own sense of purpose and rightness.*

Only when you feel threatened do you feel the need to defend. Notice that when you feel you need to defend something, it probably wasn't securely yours, or you wouldn't feel so defensive.

This is a helpful way to monitor your feelings about what you truly own and what you feel you need to fight for. The soul's way of protecting what it owns is inherent. All that it knows itself to be, it will protect, gently and lovingly. The ego's way is jealous and defensive.

When you begin to feel your soul guiding you, give thanks to it for its light and love.

When you begin to feel the ego taking charge, gently go within and claim for yourself whatever it is you felt you needed to fight for. Fighting will never lead you to peace. Like attracts like. To have peace, be peace. To have gentle power, be gentle power. No one will pull you out of your chair and say, "Okay, use your power, come on, use it," unless you have a really good friend. If not, or when that friend is pulling herself or himself out of their chair, you will have to be your own best friend. If you are unsatisfied with anything at anytime, it is simply a misdirection of energy, which you have chosen to use thusly and can now choose to harness, claim, and direct otherwise.

Ether is the energy surrounding the planet that has within it all of the memories of all that has happened emotionally, physically, mentally, and spiritually on the planet, which is why peaceful visualization of the planet is so powerful. The magnetic vibration of your thoughts attracts and strengthens the already existing thoughts of peace. If we surround our planet with loving thoughts and actions, and peace-filled vibrations, we make the force-field that much stronger.

Spiritual growth involves increasing your aware-ness that we are all one, and that when you send out light to another, you are also sending it to yourself. It involves increasing your awareness of beauty, opening your heart and experiencing more love, compassion, and acceptance of people for where they are, allow-ing you to accept yourself for where you are. The judgements you place on others come from the judge-ments you place on yourself.

Free others, and you will free yourself. Free yourself, and you will free others. You are one.

CHAPTER 5
IN THE COURAGE IT COMES

You all have shadows or you would not have chosen to be here on Earth. In fact you have chosen your shadows. The important thing is that you look at them with good cheer (God cheer). This life is like a game and you are here not only to grow but to grow graciously and with good humour and compassion and love and peace; and its okay to feel anger and sadness and love and confusion. Just deeply acknowledge that you are God feeling these things and oh! the wonder that then moves in when you know that you have a very powerful part in this life. Whomever you may be, YOU ARE IMPORTANT! The more power you allow your growth to have, the more enlivened the growth becomes and the 'enlivenedness' is the dance — the dance of the divine spark manifest in form. So, love more! Love, move, and be, knowing that you too are so totally loved, protected and guided, have always been and will always be!

The beautiful thing about life is that it is everchanging; it is a dance.

You, too, are everchanging and must allow yourself to join the dance. This means that at times you will choose to be alone, and at other times you will choose to be with others. Receiving love and support from others can mean that they leave you alone when that is appropriate.

Trust your universe.

There is one necessity involved with any path of awakening you may choose and that is total trust in your universe.

The more you commit yourself and your time to trusting and to looking for love, you shall find it. Love and faith are the very essence of who you are. It is the energy that touches you through your heart center and enlivens all of your being to a soft singing. Love answers all prayers and like attracts like. The more you intentionally look for love, the more love you shall attract. Look around you. See only love and you shall find only love.

Surrendering to your highest good takes total trust and courage. But in so doing, you will no longer need to swim upstream.

Begin to watch where your own river of energy flows, and allow this natural rhythm.

Begin to follow. . . yourself. You know, more than anyone else, what is right for you, and isn't that wonderful.

You are a part of God. That is not to say that the God Force does not exist without you acknowledging that you are a part of it. It is to say that while you are in the physical, the way to God is through your inner being, through you! Again you hear that it is not outside of you. The simple task lies in trusting this.

Those who trust this will never ask for proof, and those who do not trust will also never ask for proof. You can change no one until they are ready to change themselves. This moment with all of its seeming imperfections, is perfect.

You are never given anything you are not ready for.

Every moment is just as it should be. Trust and rejoice in that.

Trust and courage are two energies that are so vital a part of your transformation process. Someone has told you that this beautifully carved piece of wood when bowed shall make music. You admire the wood, the feel, the smell, the beauty, and you do not touch! It is one thing to know that the violin can make music. It is another to pick it up and, out of the depths of your soul and the power of spirit within you, begin the song that will take you home.

This is what the divine asks of you: to play, to dance, to rejoice. This takes total movement. And the movement takes total trust and courage. It is the trust and the courage that distinguishes a non-filled being from a wonder-filled, beautiful, creative, alive being!

Those of you who have begun to share your light and your wisdom, it is important to understand that whatever you may share from you heart in good intentions, stands as some of the most potent and important information and gift that you can give to another. Trust yourself.

The light that you speak so much of, and on beautiful occasions, feel so much of, is ever shining for you. The light truly is your saviour as you go about your journey. It is your memory of a time when you claimed and trusted your wholeness, when you were filled with wonder and dance and spontaneity, because you knew who you were. You knew yourself to be the Divine in action.

Soon, very soon, this familiar power and wonder shall be reclaimed in order to heal the mother earth. She is shifting ever so surely to regain this balance and this knowing and to teach it to her children. You as her child are a beautiful and very important part of this balance. In essence, the balance and knowing and light has always been with you. You have chosen to mistrust it at times because you believed that the physical world alone would hold greater gifts than the Divine, than the Mother and Father themselves. You have now decided to lend a hand to your own transformation. You are so filled with inner memory.

*Going home to reach
the beginning . . .*

CHAPTER 6
WHAT HAS
MADE THEM MASTERS?

The masters, or enlightened beings, all had and still have (for they live on) one common thread and choose to manifest it in very different ways, appealing to different-natured people in different ways. That thread is courage; the courage to look beyond the ordinary, to see beneath the words and cries of their brothers and sisters and deep, deep into the heart of the matter. They saw that when they dared to go deep enough, everyone was the same. All else aside, what was left was deep, abiding, strong, courageous love. It is to this part of your being that the masters spoke.

They came as examples, yet they were not essentially different from you and me. The only difference was that they saw the love and had the courage to say, "I recognize you as spiritual light and it is to this wise part of you that I shall speak; and if you cannot hear me now, come back when you can, because I shall be waiting." They do not give up or turn their backs.

They are not gone when they leave the physical vehicle. They are holding to their divine promise; they will be waiting.

The masters are ready to reflect the deep, wise, wondrous part of your being, when you are ready to show that part.

The job of the masters is that of reflection, which means that in the end, you will have to lean on no one, including the masters and great beings. They are here to remind you that inside of you lies everything you have ever wanted, ever looked for, and ever believed was outside of you. They are here to say, "go within." That is where the courage comes in on your part.

The masters are in the ethers and can be called upon at any time you choose. Exchange between spirits and spirits in bodies is much older than the earth it-self. The masters are emissaries of light in service to the divine, and they only want one basic thing from each of you, and that basic thing is to know who you are and to stand by it! The divine sends these masters in deep hope that they will spark a light in each one of you, and this is why the divine sends so many, all saying different spiritual paths will lead you home. And they will!

If you would really take the time to go deeper with any path you choose, you would know that they all lead home.

Therein lies the beauty which you have perceived as, and made into, the separation. Separation, in truth, does not exist. You have created separation in your mind, and if you would take up the 'wooden vio-lin' and just begin to play a few sounds, the rest of your world would begin to resonate as well.

45

*Your entire reality is created
by your perceptions, and
those perceptions are created
entirely by you.*

It is one of the deepest understandings you could
have about living life on planet earth, and in other
realms as well.

*Out of deep respect for you,
the Creator has given you
the freedom to do with your
life and your perceptions
as you wish, knowing that
your true essence is love.*

So in the end, you cannot be anything but loving.
It is what you gravitate towards; it is what you look
for in the eyes of another, and in your own being. If

you ever see any action that is not loving, it is simply a cry for love, our essence.

When you begin to get quiet within, you tap your true roots of love.

The essence of any one of your paths is telling you to fill yourself with life, to love with right action, and not to depend on another's words, including the masters', until you have made them your own through your own sweet will to be loving and full.

Today, tomorrow, and forever, reach your soul and come from within. Feel your heart. Grow with love and become love, the simple, pure, delicate gem.

47

CHAPTER 7
JOYOUS HEALING ENERGIES

To touch the earth with its own language of sound, tone, color, and vibration, makes you one again — as you have always been and have sometimes remembered.

The colors you are drawn to are the ones which heal you the most. Clear crystalline holds the essence of transcendence, transformation, receiving guidance from higher realms, spontaneity, and divine order. It relates to your crown chakra. Violet holds the essence of introspection, meditation, intuition, and knowledge. It relates to your third eye chakra. Gold holds the essence of wisdom, ritual, and splendor and relates to all chakras. The essence of communication of deepest truths, of self-worth, and of calmness are held in blue. Blue relates to the throat chakra. Green holds the essence of healing, soothing, and of peace. Green relates to the heart chakra. The essence of self love, spiritual love, acceptance, surrender, non-judgement, and tenderness are held in pink. Pink relates to the heart chakra. Orange holds the essence of personality, of transformation, and of change. It relates to the solar plexus chakra and to the second chakra. Red is the holder of the essence of life force, of vitality and manifesting. Red relates to the base chakra. The essence of grounding, nurturing, and growth are held within black. It relates to the base chakra.

It is interesting to observe the colors you wear the most, have in your home environment the most, as well as in your work environment. When you avoid a color, you are usually avoiding the essences of that color.

Chakras are wheels of energy in our etheric body and in the etheric body of the Mother Earth. Each one of our chakras governs particular aspects of being, emotional, physical, and spiritual. The chakras are subtle, powerful, and beautiful. One way to become in touch with these energies in your life, is to sit and begin to feel their movement, their vibration in your own etheric, or energy body. You receive so many messages all of the time through these energy centers. Your relaxed concentration upon them will greatly aid you in realizing how these divine energies are moving in your etheric vibrational body.

We live in a world of vibration. We are made of vibration and it is to vibration we shall return. Music is the gentle awakener. Music lets you feel lively, sacred, joyful, sad, and beautiful emotions, all of which are already inside of you. Music simply allows your wholeness to emerge naturally, and without judgement or force, you become your higher or soul self. God blessed us with music; it is blessing in action. Watch it carry you. Watch it transform you. It is magic, it is communication of the heart.

The beauty of the natural world around you is also your healer.

All you truly need is yourself and the willingness to be healed, and the doors begin to swing open.

The inherent power of nature has long been used and understood by people of great depth and wisdom.

AWAKENING

There is a very unique feeling of expansiveness and connectedness, when you spend some time with the mountains, with the trees, with a river. These things are symbols of your own vastness. They represent the purity within, and the deep sense of patience and flow that lies within you. The stillness of the mountains, of the trees, of the river, even while it flows, of the sky, are some of the best teachers you have. Crystals, too, are forms of great beauty and wisdom. The crystals are tools — tools which help you to reflect a greater depth within, as do the mountains and the sky. Crystals amplify your energy, your beliefs, your light, and that puts the responsibility back to you. You energize the crystals. They are visual forms, gifts from the divine, to remind you of your inner power and light. They are a tool to go beyond, to reach the essence of what they reflect, and that is you and your light.

Watch the seasons. They represent the changes you go through, each one unique and elegant unto itself, as well as together. The seasons teach you to live in the moment while existing in a world of infinite moments. You are a wondrous facet of the divine. When you know deep in your being that you are a part of God, you know your sisters and brothers to be all around you and you begin to have loving insight into all beings and all aspects of life.

CHAPTER 8
LOVE: OUR ESSENCE

*You are that
very loving essence
for which you seek.*

Elizabeth Joy is an author, an artist, and a teacher. She brings to her work a rich background of metaphysics and spirituality. Elizabeth believes that within each person lies infinite love, wisdom, inspiration and joy, and that these gifts are expressed when each person chooses to awaken to them. Her books and tapes reflect this belief.

Other books by Elizabeth Joy:

LIVING A JOYOUS LIFE